SCENIC
KwaZulu-Natal

SUNBIRD PUBLISHERS

2 4 6 8 10 9 7 5 3 1
First Published 2006
Sunbird Publishers (Pty) Ltd
P O Box 6836, Roggebaai, 8012 Cape Town, South Africa

www.sunbirdpublishers.co.za

Registration number: 4850177827
Copyright © 2006 published edition: Sunbird Publishers
Copyright © 2006 text: Pat de la Harpe
Copyright © 2006 photographs: Roger de la Harpe

Publisher Natanya Mulholland
Editor Sean Fraser
Designer Mandy McKay
Production Manager Andrew de Kock

Reproduction by Unifoto (Pty) Ltd, Cape Town
Printed and bound by Tien Wah Press (Pte) Ltd, Singapore

ISBN 1 919 93841 9

TO ANITA AND JOHN, WITH LOVE

TITLE PAGE *The setting sun leaves a shimmering trail across the tranquil waters of Lake St Lucia.*
LEFT *A young Zulu warrior wields his shield and spear as generations have done before him.*
ABOVE *Mist envelopes the rocks and grass at Giant's Castle in the Drakensberg.*
OPPOSITE *The Tugela Falls, the world's second highest, plunge a spectacular 900 metres.*
OVERLEAF *The Valley of a Thousand Hills stretches as far as the horizon and beyond.*

KwaZulu-Natal – Kingdom of the Zulu

ABOVE *The Maputaland Marine Reserve begins just north of Sodwana Bay and continues all the way to the Mozambique border. This pristine stretch of coastal reserve includes the adjacent area offshore, extending three nautical miles into the sea.*

Washed by the warm waters of the Indian Ocean on the eastern side of South Africa, KwaZulu-Natal sweeps through tropical beaches, rolling green hills, the lofty crags of the mighty Drakensberg and the incredible biodiversity of some of Africa's oldest game reserves. Its landscapes embrace two of South Africa's World Heritage Sites – the magnificent uKhahlamba-Drakensberg Park and the unique estuarine system of the Greater St Lucia Wetland Park.

Traditional home of the Zulu people, KwaZulu-Natal is widely recognised as the Kingdom of the Zulu. Many of its towns and rivers boast historical Zulu names and at its heart lies the vibrant city of Durban, or eThekweni, which beats with a rhythm of its own. Here sights, sounds and smells assault the senses in a multicultural bustle of formal and informal traders, markets and restaurants in an eclectic mix of Western, Asian and African styles.

The city's colonial past is unmistakeable, its wide streets dotted with old buildings and quaint shops that reflect the influence of both European and Indian architectural trends. Indeed, Durban has become the place to view Art Deco architecture at its best, along with several fine examples of churches, mosques and temples.

Durban is Africa's busiest port and the lively area near the harbour mouth provides an exciting setting for flea markets, dockside bistros and restaurants. It is here, too, that you will find the best fish and chips in town. The largest aquarium in the southern hemisphere can be found at the huge theme park, uShaka Marine World, along with a variety of thrilling water rides, restaurants, art galleries and shops. The harbour has its own vibrancy, hosting huge ships and freighters from around the world, while smaller boats huddle together at several quays along the Victoria Embankment.

A number of piers used by both anglers and strollers jut out into the bay, where endless beaches are the city's greatest attraction. Along the famous 'Golden Mile' up-market hotels with superb ocean views jostle for space with sidewalk cafés, amusement parks and swimming pools. Here curio sellers and craft markets add to an energetic buzz that is typically Durban in style.

To the south of KwaZulu-Natal's leisure capital, across the Umkomaas River, is a stretch of coastline famous for its beaches, lagoons and vibey holiday towns. Like Durban, this seafront – known as the South Coast by locals – enjoys warm weather year round and attracts sun seekers in their thousands, particularly during the peak school holiday periods in April, July and December.

Fields of sugar cane, banana plantations and luxuriant indigenous bush vie for space between the villages that hug the beaches and rocky coves. Hibberdene, Uvongo, Margate, Ramsgate and Port Shepstone are but a few of the seaside towns that offer affordable relaxation and adventure. Cafés, restaurants, bars and shops, as well as golden beaches and warm seas cater for most tastes, while an impressive number of golf courses – 11 in total – attract an endless stream of golfing enthusiasts. Surfing, snorkelling and scuba diving are particularly popular and the fishing is exceptional, especially when the shad are running.

The annual Sardine Run, however, leads to a greater frenzy of excitement. In June or July each year, millions of sardines migrate up the South Coast in huge shoals before heading out to sea. Their progress is monitored by a fascinated public and when some shoals beach, they are met by exuberant crowds who throw all dignity to the wind and scoop the sardines up in their thousands, carrying the fish off in anything that will contain them, including shirt and trouser pockets and even raised skirts. This massive sardine migration is believed to be unique, the spectacle made even more fascinating by the accompaniment of hundreds of sharks, dolphins and whales that feast on these little fish for weeks, but appear to make no dent in their numbers.

There are several nature reserves on the South Coast that are well worth a visit and, like most of Kwa-Zulu-Natal's reserves, are run by the province's nature conservation body, Ezemvelo KZN Wildlife. Inland from the coastal village of Park Rynie is the Vernon Crookes Nature Reserve, which offers magnificent views across undulating hills. It is home to several species of antelope, zebra, wildebeest and a significant bird population, the latter attracted to the reserve's coastal forests and rolling grasslands.

Further south towards Port Shepstone, the uMzimkulwana River, over millennia, has worn through layers of sandstone to produce the dramatic Oribi Gorge. Plunging cliffs, forested

ABOVE *The undulating slopes of the Little 'Berg in the Giant's Castle area provide ample opportunity for game- and bird-watching, especially during the summer months when grasses and flowering shrubs flourish in the valleys.*

ABOVE *Intrepid hikers cross the Pholela River near Cobham in the southern Drakensberg.*

slopes and waterfalls form cool green glades – much to the delight of the rare samango monkeys that inhabit the area. Reedbuck, bushbuck, the blue and common duiker, as well as baboons and vervet monkeys are also found here. Some 270 bird species have been recorded, with good sightings of raptors, especially the crowned, long-crested and black eagles.

The Umtamvuna Nature Reserve is KwaZulu-Natal's southernmost reserve. Located near Port Edward on the Mtamvuna River, it is particularly scenic, consisting largely of a deep gorge covered with indigenous forest. About 1 300 plant species have been documented, including 25 different varieties of orchids. There is a large breeding colony of Cape vultures, and the rare peregrine falcon and Gurney's sugarbird can also be seen. Several antelope species occur here, including bushbuck, reedbuck and both the common and blue duiker.

To the north of Durban lies the so-called North Coast, which stretches past the mighty Thukela (Tugela) River and beyond. Parts of this coastline are favoured by the bottlenosed dolphin – large schools may be seen cavorting or occasionally

feeding in the shallows. Sweeping white beaches, lagoons and tidal pools interspersed with up-market resort towns are characteristic of this coastal strip, as are the vast fields of sugar cane further inland. The beaches along this coastline are quite distinct from those further south in that they have some of the highest vegetated dunes in the world.

The holiday towns of Umhlanga Rocks, Umdloti and Ballito are particularly popular with those holidaymakers on the lookout for fabulous beaches with ample facilities and leisure activities. Luxurious hotels and apartments line the beachfront, while sidewalk cafés, restaurants and shops abound. Surfing, wind surfing and fishing, as well as reef snorkelling and scuba diving, are favourite pastimes. Several scenic golf courses are within easy reach too – some offering spectacular greens punctuated by stands of indigenous bush, which attract a diversity of bird life.

Further north lies the little town of Mtunzini, situated on the banks of the Mlalazi River. It has excellent fishing, a wonderful beach and the intriguing Umlalazi Nature Reserve.

The reserve covers several hectares of dune forest as well as mangrove swamp, accessible via a number of walking trails that zigzag through a range of ecosystems. The short trail leading through the mangrove swamp is a muddy experience, but is well worth the effort, as several crab species, the curious mudskipper fish and a type of tree-climbing whelk are easily spotted. Vervet monkeys are common in the reserve, while its other residents, the shy bushbuck and red and blue duiker, are only occasionally spotted. The bird life is abundant and varied and the rare palmnut vulture is found here, attracted to the raffia palms growing in the surrounding coastal forests.

Still further north is South Africa's first proclaimed World Heritage Site, The Greater St Lucia Wetland Park, which extends all the way up to the Mozambique border. Over

ABOVE The endangered wild dog was reintroduced to the Hluhluwe-Imfolozi Park in the 1980s and numbers have increased steadily.

a quarter of a million hectares in extent, it is the largest estuarine system in Africa and incorporates an incredible range of habitats, from vast stretches of beach to swamps, freshwater lakes, undulating grasslands, forests and bushveld. The resultant diversity of animal and bird life is spectacular.

From Maphelane Nature Reserve in the south the park sweeps through the St Lucia Estuary, False Bay Park, Cape Vidal, Sodwana Bay, Mkhuze Game Reserve and on to the Maputaland Marine Reserve and Kosi Bay. This area was considerably different some 140 million years ago when it was submerged beneath the sea. Through the centuries, the level of the oceans fluctuated, gradually creating sandstone outcrops where the surf zone is today. Over the millennia, sand was slowly deposited on these outcrops, forming the huge vegetated dunes that are so characteristic of the area today. Ancient rivers meandered through a vast floodplain and, on meeting the coastal dunes, dammed up and formed a shallow system of lakes and pans. Numerous fossil remains of marine animals, such as pectin clams, belemnites and ammonites, have been found, many discovered considerable distances away from the present seashore.

The estuary is shallow – a mere one metre deep on average – although several deeper channels do occur. Significant populations of hippo and crocodile are found in and around the lake system – reportedly the greatest congregation of these two species in South Africa. The waters are rich in crustaceans, fish and other organisms, which provide a year-round food source for many thousands of water birds and waders. About 60 per cent of South Africa's Caspian terns breed here and, in autumn, as many as 6 000 white pelicans arrive to take advantage of the schools of mullet that move into the narrows before heading out to sea to spawn. The pelicans, as well as other birds such as greyheaded gulls, redwinged pratincoles and African spoonbills, make use of several islands in the lake on which to breed. Indeed, some 420 species of bird have been recorded in the area.

ABOVE A young Zulu girl proudly shows off her bead accessories. Today, traditional dress remains a vital part of local ceremonies.

The town of St Lucia is situated on the banks of the estuary and offers a variety of accommodation, restaurants and shops. Fishing is almost a religion in these parts, enthusiasts fishing in both the lake and the sea. Launch tours on the estuary are an ideal way to enjoy the hippo, crocodile and bird populations, and provide splendid views of the surrounds. Ezemvelo KZN Wildlife has set out numerous walks and hiking trails that vary in length and difficulty and encompass various points of interest around the lake.

The Crocodile Centre gives visitors an educational look at these amazing – and ancient – reptiles and is especially interesting at feeding times.

The road from St Lucia to the magnificent beach at Cape Vidal traverses the so-called Eastern Shores where rolling grassland and coastal forests are home to a variety of antelope, zebra, warthog, black and white rhino and elephant, the latter recently reintroduced to the area after an absence of some 100 years. The white sands of Cape Vidal's beach are quite breathtaking and stretch for miles to the north and south.

Swimming, fishing and snorkelling are excellent in the protected bay and several trails wind their way through the dune forests. There are also two whale and dolphin lookout platforms, the whale sightings being particularly good during June and July. In the forests, red duiker, warthog, bushbuck and the rare samango monkey occur, while the bird life is prolific. The area is also home to hippo and a wary eye should be kept open for these often volatile animals.

Sodwana Bay is renowned for having the southernmost tropical coral reefs in Africa and scuba divers from around the world come to enjoy this underwater paradise. A kaleidoscope of colourful reef fish, whales, sharks and rays, as well as no fewer than 95 species of corals and sponges can be seen beneath the surface. Several specimens of the coelacanth, previously thought to be extinct, have been sighted here and have increased the importance of this marine sanctuary. Game fish, too, are abundant and deep-sea fishing expeditions are a regular feature of the area.

Perhaps the most intriguing phenomenon, however, is the arrival on this coastline of the enormous leatherback and loggerhead turtles between October and February each year. The females return to the same stretch of beach where they

ABOVE *Guests enjoy a magnificent sunset over the lake system at Kosi Bay. At most tourist venues in the area guides are drawn from the local community and their knowledge of the surrounds is extensive.*

ABOVE *The tented camp at Mkhuze has a 'safari' ambiance. Nyala, kudu and other antelope are often spotted in the camp.*

themselves were born, emerging from the sea at night to nest and lay their eggs above the high-water mark. The eggs of both species hatch about 65 days later and, as the hatchlings make their way to the sea, many fall prey to ghost crabs and sea birds. Those that reach the sea are swept by currents to the south where they spend some 15 years before reaching sexual maturity. Then, incredibly, instinct drives the females – like their mothers before them – to return to the same beach to nest. These fascinating creatures can be seen on special turtle tours run by Ezemvelo KZN Wildlife as well as several private tour operators during December and January.

Pristine beaches stretch for kilometres, reaching the truly fabulous Kosi Bay area on the border with Mozambique. Kosi Bay is a unique ecosystem that consists of a series of four lakes, ranging from freshwater to saline, which are separated from the ocean by forested sand dunes, eventually feeding into the sea through a narrow mouth. Hippo inhabit the lake system, while the mangrove swamps, marshes and fig forests provide a habitat for a variety of other creatures, from samango

monkey to bushpig, as well as an abundant bird life, the endangered palmnut vulture being a resident here.

The local Tonga people have developed an ingenious way of catching fish in the lakes, using traps made from reeds. These unique traps are part of ancient Tonga tradition and are built to form enclosures that hold the fish when the tide recedes. Each trap remains the property of the family concerned and is handed down from father to son through the generations.

Further inland, away from the shoreline but also part of the Greater St Lucia Wetland Park, is the Mkhuze Game Reserve. Its woodland savanna is dotted with thorn trees, thickets, riverine forest and an extensive stand of sycamore figs. It is home to a variety of antelope, black and white rhino, giraffe, zebra, wildebeest, leopard and elephant, while lion are shortly to be reintroduced. There are several game-viewing hides located at various water holes and at the Nsumu Pan, which plays host to a large number of hippo and crocodile and hundreds of birds. The viewing hides are especially

ABOVE *Lush green fields of sugar cane are a feature of both the North and South Coasts of KwaZulu-Natal.*

productive during the rather dry winter months when game sightings in the region can be quite spectacular.

In the far north, both the Tembe Elephant Reserve and the Ndumo Game Reserve butt up against Mozambique and

ABOVE *In spring, the grassy slopes of the Umgeni Valley Nature Reserve in the Midlands are dotted with colourful indigenous flowers.*

are part of a planned Transfrontier Park that will incorporate large tracts of land on both sides of the Mozambique/South African border. Tembe Elephant Reserve, named after the Tembe clan who traditionally live in this area, was established to protect the last remaining herds of elephant that migrate between the two countries. Previously decimated by relentless poaching, the elephants now thrive and their numbers have increased dramatically. Dense stands of woodland cover the area and although game-viewing is difficult, it is particularly rewarding, as the elephants are impressive in stature, with exceptionally large tusks. The small Ndumo Game Reserve has several sizeable pans, surrounded by fever trees and fig tree woodlands, and is an ornithologist's delight. Many species of bird, at the most southern limit of their range, occur here and sightings include the Pel's fishing owl, narina trogan and brown-headed parrot.

The Hluhluwe-Imfolozi Park is located in an area rich in Zulu history and tradition. Founded in 1895, the reserve is the largest in the province and one of the oldest in Africa, its diverse scenery part of its unique attraction. Hluhluwe, in the north, has steep forested hills with grassy slopes, while riverine woodland lines the Hluhluwe River and other watercourses. Moving south and west towards Imfolozi, the terrain becomes flatter and drier, and savanna woodland and open grasslands cover large areas. Few of the rivers contain permanent water in this section and even the White and Black Umfolozi Rivers sometimes stop flowing during very dry periods.

Herds of antelope, giraffe, wildebeest, zebra and the Big Five – lion, elephant, buffalo, rhino and leopard – can be seen in the park, and their are good sightings of cheetah, wild dog and spotted hyena, amongst others, too. The bird life is abundant and more than 400 species have been recorded here. The reserve is world renowned for its role in saving the white rhino from extinction and you are almost assured of spotting these huge beasts. Relocation of white, and to a lesser extent black rhino, to other protected areas in Africa has proved very

ABOVE *Although not one of the ever-favourite Big Five, cheetah are a popular attraction in KwaZulu-Natal's parks and reserves.*

successful and it is said that almost every white rhino on the continent today can trace its origins back to this reserve.

As elsewhere, game-viewing is particularly rewarding during the dry winter months when the grass is short and the scarcity of water forces the animals to make their way to the various water holes and rivers to drink. Ezemvelo KZN Wildlife conducts several walking trails through the Imfolozi wilderness area, the trails varying in length from a few hours to several days. Night drives are available from the two main camps, Hilltop in Hluhluwe and Mpila in Imfolozi. There are several areas where visitors can stop and picnic and enjoy the tranquillity of nature, as well as various lookout sites that offer superb views over the reserve.

Close to the town of Vryheid, once the scene of violent clashes during the turbulent war years, is the serenely scenic Ithala Game Reserve, a rugged and beautiful reserve that drops off the escarpment to the Pongola River through a series of rocky hills and open grasslands. Previously farmed,

Ithala has been successfully restocked with game, some of which had become extinct in the area. Several species of antelope, giraffe, wildebeest, black and white rhino, warthog, cheetah, brown hyena, leopard and elephant have found a home here, while the Pongola River harbours many crocodiles. The abundant bird life is attracted to the variety of habitats, and the cliffs above Ntshondwe Camp are the favourite nesting sites of black eagles. The game viewing is rewarding and Ezemvelo KZN Wildlife conducts day walks and wilderness trails through the reserve.

Pietermaritzburg, capital of KwaZulu-Natal, lies some 90 kilometres inland from Durban. Its colonial past is easily recognisable and some grand old Victorian and Edwardian buildings stand cheek by jowl with their more modern counterparts. The city is the gateway to the Midlands, an area of small farming towns, lush green hills, fields and pastures, forests and trout dams. There are numerous waterfalls and streams, the Karkloof and Howick Falls being especially spectacular. The uMgeni River, which forms the Howick Falls as it plunges some 100 metres into the gorge below, also feeds the huge Midmar Dam – a beautiful venue for yachting and watersport enthusiasts, as well as a place to picnic and relax.

ABOVE Ndumo Game Reserve in the far north of the province has extensive stands of fever trees, the almost luminous yellow bark their most outstanding feature. These trees are especially prolific at the spectacular Nyamithi Pan.

ABOVE The haunting cry of the African fish eagle is characteristic of many of KwaZulu-Natal's reserves and conservation areas.

The Midlands Meander, a highly successful arts-and-crafts-route, stretches across the Midlands in a network of country roads. It incorporates not only crafts in the more conventional sense but also offers cheese-making, beer brewing, nature reserves, herb gardens, indigenous nurseries, country inns, restaurants, hikes, horse-riding, trout-fishing and mountain-biking.

The province's other World Heritage Site, the impressive uKhahlamba-Drakensberg Park, lies in the west, the massive Drakensberg range forming the border between KwaZulu-Natal and the Kingdom of Lesotho. The Drakensberg is the highest range of mountains in South Africa and soars to an incredible 3 482 metres. These mountains attract hikers, birders and nature lovers from around the world, lured by the tranquillity and majesty of the surrounds.

The basalt peaks and buttresses of the High 'Berg offer the most dramatic vistas, their rugged contours giving rise to names like Cathedral Peak, The Pudding, The Bell, Monk's Cowl and Giant's Castle. These craggy heights provide a home to numerous raptors, including the rare lammergeier, or bearded vulture, and these magnificent birds can sometimes be spotted flying the thermals. The Amphitheatre in the northern 'Berg, dominated by the Mont-aux-Sources peak, is particular spectacular and it is here that the powerful Thukela River tumbles an awesome 900 metres down the escarpment. The foothills of the mountains – generally known as the Little 'Berg – lie below 2 000 metres and are characterised by grassy slopes and valleys cut by cold mountain streams and rivers. The local trout dams are particularly popular with fly fishermen. A variety of antelope, most especially mountain reedbuck and eland, are found on the lower slopes, while the bird life is prolific.

The Drakensberg's sandstone base has eroded over many millennia to form numerous caves and overhangs, some of which were inhabited by South Africa's original inhabitants, the San (Bushmen), who left behind a priceless legacy of rock art – a visual documentary of their lifestyle, beliefs and ceremonies through the centuries. It is thanks to these people that the Drakensberg has been hailed as the largest open-air art gallery in the world. The most outstanding rock art sites are very accessible to the average visitor. These include the art found in the Main Caves at Giant's Castle as well as that of the magnificent Game Pass Shelter at Kamberg. The San Rock Art Interpretive Centre at Didima Camp in the Cathedral Peak area provides fascinating insights into the lives of these gentle people.

History in the making

Zululand's turbulent past is buried beneath gently rolling hills and grasslands, the lush valleys and plains dotted with Zulu homesteads. Before the Zulu king Shaka seized power in 1816, the Zulu people were one of many different clans living between the Drakensberg and the Indian Ocean. Land for grazing their cattle was in short supply and this led to frequent clashes between the various groups. In the 12 years of his reign, Shaka led his men in a series of bloody battles against rival tribes and succeeded in uniting them under his

ABOVE *Fishing at St Lucia – from lake, shore and sea – is extremely rewarding and a pastime taken very seriously by enthusiasts.*

ABOVE *The rolling hills of the KwaZulu-Natal Midlands offer spectacular views of lush green fields, big skies, picturesque farmhouses and peacefully grazing cattle. The region is also home to the very popular arts-and-crafts route – The Midlands Meander.*

rule. In so doing, he forged the Zulu nation and, at the same time, created one of the most powerful military forces in all of Africa. He called his kingdom 'KwaZulu', which means 'Place of the People of the Heavens', and indeed it is a paradise, offering breathtaking views, panoramic vistas and huge blue skies.

In spite of the powerful influences of Westernisation, many of the old traditions and customs are retained in rural Zululand today. Zulu folklore is rich in references to wild animals and nature, and names and proverbs with their roots in the natural world are still used extensively. As in the past, cattle remain an obsession and the Nguni breed in particular is highly prized. They are not only a visible measure of a man's wealth but without them he cannot marry as the *lobolo*, or bride price, is paid in cattle.

Zulu ceremonies are vibrant and colourful, providing a spectacular showpiece of traditional dance and dress. Magnificent beadwork made into necklaces, headdresses and belts offset the use of animal skins and cow tails. Dancing, singing and the beating of drums play a major role at these gatherings, the dancing in particular being very energetic.

The men carry shields, spears and sticks, which they use to great effect during their performances, their movements usually illustrating battle or hunting scenes. The women's dancing is equally vigorous and, like the men, they kick and stamp their feet to the beat of drums, in a display of steps and routines handed down through generations.

Aside from the violent upheavals of Shaka's rule, Zululand was to know even more bloodshed when it was invaded by the Boers and then the British. This area, as well as the northern parts of KwaZulu-Natal, was the scene of some of the most turbulent years in South Africa's history, and cost the lives of Boer, Brit and Zulu in a series of bloody confrontations between 1836 and 1902. The region has the highest number of battlefields in South Africa, drawing visitors from around the world. Those towns that are encompassed by the various sites have banded together to form what is today known as the Battlefields Route. There are museums and interpretive displays at several of the battle sites, and the publicity offices in the surrounding towns offer information on all the battles as well as suggestions on accommodation, historical guides, self-guided tours and trails.

The establishment of British rule in the Cape Colony in 1806 caused widespread discontent among the Boers, who viewed the advent of the British as a threat to their culture and language. As a result, they set out from the Cape in their thousands to seek greener pastures in the interior in a mass exodus between 1836 and 1852 that became known in the history books as the Great Trek. After an epic journey across the mighty Drakensberg, one party of trekkers, led by a man called Piet Retief, arrived in the Zulu Kingdom in 1837. He duly initiated negotiations with Dingane, Shaka's brother and successor, for land on which to settle. Before the agreement could be ratified, however, Dingane had Piet Retief and several of his men killed. This was the start of a series of bitter battles between the Boers and the Zulus, particularly in the area near the present-day town of Estcourt. Then, in late 1838, the trekkers regrouped and moved further north to avenge the death of their people. On 16 December 1838, at the Battle of Blood River – today more commonly known as Ncome, especially by the Zulu people themselves – the Boers successfully repulsed an attack by the Zulu army and Dingane was forced to flee.

ABOVE Trailists in the Imfolozi are accompanied by a game ranger, while their belongings are sent ahead on donkeys.

Dingane was succeeded by King Mpande and for the 32 years of his reign relative peace descended on the area. Mpande, in turn, was succeeded by his son Cetshwayo, who set about strengthening the Zulu Kingdom that had grown soft from years of inactivity. Cetshwayo's actions were, however, viewed as a threat by the British colonialists in the neighbouring Natal Colony and an ultimatum was presented to the Zulu king, the conditions of which were impossible to meet. On expiry of the ultimatum in January 1879, British troops invaded Zululand and the first engagements of the Anglo-Zulu War took place at Isandlwana and Rorke's Drift. The British regiments were almost completely annihilated at the Battle of Isandlwana by a force of some 25 000 Zulus, their defeat a total humiliation – the first time British forces had ever been crushed by a so-called 'savage army'.

Later that same day, 22 January 1879, the British post at Rorke's Drift, manned by a handful of men left behind to guard the hospital and supplies, was attacked by an impi of about 4 000 Zulus. For 12 hours the soldiers fought off repeated attacks by the Zulu warriors and finally emerged victorious, which did much to restore British morale. This encounter led to the award of 11 Victoria Crosses, the highest number ever awarded for a single engagement. Finally, on 4 July 1879 the British defeated the Zulu army at the Battle of Ulundi, leaving the once mighty Zulu nation in a state of complete disarray.

The unsuccessful attempts by the Boers of the Transvaal Republic to regain their independence from Britain by peaceful means led to what was to become known as the First Anglo-Boer War in 1880. The British forces marched from Durban to Newcastle so as to be close to the border of the Transvaal. Numerous skirmishes erupted in the area, finally culminating in the Battle of Majuba in 1881. Resentment continued to fester between the Boers and the British, however, and war was once again declared on 11 October 1899, signalling the start of the Second Anglo-Boer War,

which raged on until 1902. This time round, the Boers of the Transvaal Republic were supported by those of the Orange Free State, and Northern Natal, which bordered on both areas, was the scene of many bloody clashes throughout the period. The Battle of Talana, just outside Dundee, saw the opening salvos of the war and was witness to the British army wearing khaki for the first time.

This then is the face of KwaZulu-Natal, a place rich in history and natural wonders, its people warmly hospitable to any who wish to explore its diverse beauty.

ABOVE This statue in Pietermaritzburg pays tribute to Gandhi, who played a pivotal role in the often troubled history of Natal.

LEFT The bright floral heads of a group of red-hot pokers stand tall against a deep blue sky. They are robust flowers and do well in higher altitudes and marshy areas and are sometimes planted close to homesteads in rural communities, supposedly to ward off lightning.

ABOVE A field of sunflowers provides a vibrant splash of bright yellow.

OPPOSITE Donkeys are regularly used to transport heavy bags of clay near Melmoth in central Zululand. The women of the community use the clay to make a variety of traditional pots to sell to the growing tourist trade in the area. It is not unusual for families to be involved in the process, the money a vital income to the household.

ABOVE A woman takes a brief break from her daily chores. The life of a Zulu woman in a traditional home is not always an easy one; she is expected to rear the children, keep the homestead tidy, cultivate the crops and collect firewood and water.

OPPOSITE A herd of cattle grazes peacefully in green pastures on the way to Injasuthi, in the Giant's Castle area of the Drakensberg. In spring these fields are sprinkled with wild flowers, while in winter they can be covered in snow.

ABOVE *Sangomas*, or diviners, are consulted on matters of misfortune, illness and the future. A few *sangomas* specialise in the use of a particular medium in order to communicate with the ancestors – a well-known diviner in the Umfolozi area of Zululand is said to use the deadly black mamba and puff adder to great effect.

ABOVE Zulu culture still places great store on physical courage and fighting ability, and traditional weapons remain an integral part of a man's attire. The art of stick fighting is learned at an early age and is in particular demand as a form of entertainment at weddings and other celebrations.

OPPOSITE Traditional family groups are large and from an early age children are taught to assist around the homestead. In spite of their many chores, the youngsters still find time to play and, like children everywhere, use whatever comes to hand to invent games. Here a group of Zulu children amuse themselves with stones and bottle caps.

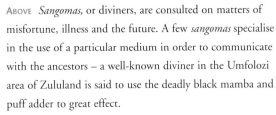

ABOVE During a wedding celebration, the families of both the bride and groom take turns to sing and dance. Personal items, such as beaded necklaces or belts, are exchanged between the families and then later returned, the interaction cementing the bonds between them. It is also an occasion for the respective kin to air any grievances they may have with each other and invariably the chosen speakers delight in the attention and shout out their comments, some of which can be quite long and involved.

OPPOSITE *Sangomas* are called to their profession by the ancestors. Most wear clothing that identifies their special status and role in the community. This can include a beaded headdress topped by the inflated bladders of sacrificed animals, or the feathers of various birds. *Sangomas* usually carry a whisk made from the tail of the blue wildebeest, which is a powerful symbol of their abilities. They often work in close association with *inyangas*, or traditional healers, who concoct herbal remedies for the treatment of illnesses.

ABOVE The Battle of Isandlwana, which took place on 22 January 1879, saw the defeat of the British army by a force of 25 000 Zulu warriors. The British soldiers were buried where they fell, their graves marked by cairns of white stones, many of which remain in place today as tragic reminders of this turbulent period of KwaZulu-Natal's history.

OPPOSITE With defeat inevitable, it became imperative for Her Majesty's soldiers to save the Queen's Colour. Attempting to do so, Lieutenants Coghill and Melville were killed crossing the Buffalo River, along with several other fugitives, at a point in the river that became known as Fugitives' Drift.

ABOVE Some survivors from the Battle of Isandlwana managed to reach the British post at Rorke's Drift, which was manned by a handful of men left behind to guard the supplies and the hospital. On hearing the news of the British defeat, the men decided to defend their post, which was attacked later that day by some 4 000 Zulu warriors. The story of how 100 soldiers successfully fought off repeated attacks by the Zulus for almost 12 hours was to become legendary.

LEFT The re-enactment of the Battle of Isandlwana is an annual event that draws large crowds of enthusiasts. The fact that victory and defeat occurred in a single day to both the British and the Zulus still fascinates many today. The British defeat at Isandlwana changed the course of British history, while Cetshwayo's premonition that Zulu sovereignty was irretrievably damaged by their defeat at Rorke's Drift proved all too true.

ABOVE Recently built, the Ncome Museum presents the Zulu interpretation of events that led to the Battle of Blood River between the Boers and the Zulus on 16 December 1838. The Ncome River – which, ironically, means 'The Peaceful One' – separates this museum from the Boer memorial on the other side. The Zulus were defeated by the Boers at this battle, which had its origins in the killing of the Voortrekker leader Piet Retief and some of his followers by the Zulu king Dingane several months earlier.

RIGHT The Boers of this period were tough pioneer types, looking for land on which to settle. In skirmishes with the Zulus, they often used their wagons as protection, which they positioned end to end in a circular shape known as a laager. The reconstruction of the laager on the site of the Battle of Blood River illustrates the Boer determination to fend off a charging Zulu impi.

ABOVE The view from Mpila Hill in the south of the Hluhluwe-Umfolozi Park looks out over grasslands and savanna towards the Black Umfolozi River. The Umfolozi section is drier than the north and is typical bushveld country. Acacias and aloes thrive in this rugged terrain, which saw the first wilderness trails in South Africa introduced in the 1960s. The wide banks of both the Black and White Umfolozi rivers provide ample opportunity for good game-viewing.

OPPOSITE Through the years, the white rhino has been ruthlessly hunted and poached for the sake of its horn – to such an extent that by the mid-1900s it was faced with extinction. A fight to save the white rhino was mounted in Imfolozi. The campaign became known as Operation Rhino and was so successful that the reserve was soon able to relocate some of these huge animals to other protected areas in Africa.

BELOW The common duiker is a solitary animal and is usually a grey to reddish yellow in colour. Only the males have horns, which are straight and short. They are shy and prefer areas that provide some sort of vegetation for cover, as they invariably hide if they are either frightened or disturbed. The common duiker is particularly active in the early morning and evening when it can be seen browsing on leaves or digging for roots or small insects.

OPPOSITE Ithala Game Reserve offers sweeping views over hills and valleys. It is especially rich in archaeological sites that date back to the Middle Stone Age and evidence of the San people has been found in some of its caves. Originally farmland, the reserve has been restocked with game that includes giraffe, black and white rhino, elephant, buffalo and various antelope.

LEFT Ithala's grasslands are home to a variety of plains and game where good sightings can be had of zebra, wildebeest, impala, eland and giraffe. White rhino also favour these areas, the endless plains able to accommodate their huge appetite for grass.

ABOVE Elephants are one of Africa's great beasts that most game viewers aim to see. Giants of the bush, a mature bull elephant can weigh as much as six tons. Huge amounts of food and water are needed to sustain an animal of this size – it is estimated that an adult can eat as much as 250 kilograms of grass and leaves a day and drink up to 200 litres of water.

OPPOSITE Buffalo love to wallow in the mud during the heat of the day. A herd of buffalo is usually quite placid, but lone bulls have a reputation of being cunning and bad-tempered, especially if they are injured or sick.

ABOVE A magnificent bird, the African hawk eagle occurs largely in hilly woodland areas. It loves to soar, either on its own or with another, and often flies very high. It feeds largely on birds such as guinea fowl, on mammals such as rodents and dassies, and on a variety of reptiles. It is daring and it is not uncommon for it to ambush its hapless victim.

OPPOSITE The Cape eagle owl is nocturnal and preys on insects, small mammals and birds. Its orange eyes are characteristic and, apart from its call, are perhaps the easiest way to distinguish it from the more common spotted eagle owl, which is similar in appearance but has yellow eyes. Males and females look alike and occur largely in mountainous areas.

BELOW The colourful lighthouse on the beachfront of the up-market coastal town of Umhlanga has become a rather famous landmark. The beach is superb and sun-seekers have plenty of opportunity to relax and enjoy safe swimming and fishing. This strip of water is particularly popular with surfers as the wave formation near the lighthouse is especially good. A paved promenade runs the full length of the beach, which is dotted with pavement cafés and refreshment stands.

OPPOSITE An aerial view of Umhlanga, with Durban in the distance, shows long stretches of white beaches lapped by the warm waters of the Indian Ocean. While palatial homes, exclusive hotels, apartments and restaurants vie for sea views, there are still areas where nature dominates, as at the Umhlanga Lagoon Nature Reserve. Here, a strip of sand-dune forest has been preserved and the large numbers of birds that it attracts get their chance of a place in the sun.

ABOVE The North Coast town of Ballito is renowned for its luxurious hotels and holiday apartments, which crowd around the two small bays that make up its fabulous beachfront. As in Umhlanga, a paved walkway wends its way along the edge of the beach, with strategically placed benches for those who wish to sit, watch the waves and breathe in the sea air. The two bays, a tidal pool and the presence of year-round life savers make Ballito a popular place for families with young children.

OPPOSITE In sharp contrast to the bustling holiday beaches further south, the Maputaland coastline shows no sign of the large hotels and apartment blocks that jostle for space and sea views. Its pristine beaches stretch uninterrupted as far as the eye can see and some of the highest vegetated dunes in the world occur here. Indeed, much of this coastline is a designated marine reserve.

LEFT Bottlenosed dolphins are frequently spotted along both the North and South coasts of KwaZulu-Natal. They are agile swimmers and often leap clear of the water. During the annual Sardine Run on the South Coast in June/July each year, large schools can be seen around the huge shoals of fish.

BELOW Humpbacked whales are not as common in KwaZulu-Natal's waters as their cousins, the southern right whales. The distinctive hump, which gives them their name, can be clearly seen when they swim near the surface of the water.

OPPOSITE Fishing at the small town of Mtunzini on the North Coast can be extremely rewarding, particularly from the beach at the Umlalazi Nature Reserve.

OPPOSITE LEFT The Burchell's coucal occurs throughout the province in both rural and suburban environments. It is also known as the 'rain bird' and its call seems particularly beautiful when heard just before the rain. Both male and female are relatively large birds and both have a rufous colouring on the rump and at the base of the tail.

OPPOSITE RIGHT Spottedbacked weavers build their nests in branches overhanging water, in reedbeds and in thornveld. Weaver colonies are always noisy and busy, with much activity taking place during nest-building when the female can be a hard taskmaster. Both sexes have black and yellow spots on their backs, but in the breeding season the male plumage changes to include a black mask.

ABOVE The Kurrichane thrush is a common resident in open woodland and thornveld, particularly near rivers and streams. It searches on the ground and among fallen leaves for food, usually grasshoppers, worms and spiders. Both male and female look alike.

RIGHT The turaco – perhaps more commonly known as the Knysna lourie – has a green head and body that make perfect camouflage in its preferred habitat of evergreen forests. The white markings around its eyes and on the tips of its crest are a startling contrast to the intense colour of its face. Turacos have a distinctive call and are usually found in pairs, often secretively scrambling about in trees or dense foliage.

LEFT Blackwinged stilts have long legs and a pointed bill that are ideally suited for wading and searching for food in the marshes, estuaries and other water courses it frequents. It makes a loud harsh call when startled and is fiercely defensive of its young.

BELOW The water thick-knee (previously known as the water dikkop) is found near rivers and wetlands that provide suitable cover. They usually occur in pairs and are particularly active at night when they are at their most vocal.

OPPOSITE African jacanas are instantly recognisable by their extremely long toes. They favour wetland areas that have floating vegetation, particularly waterlilies, which they walk on while they search for food.

LEFT The Nile crocodile is a highly successful survivor, having evolved some 180 million years ago. It is aquatic and cold-blooded and maintains its body heat by basking in the sun. In spite of their formidable appearance, both the male and the female make exemplary parents.

BELOW In subtropical KwaZulu-Natal, the female crocodile lays her eggs in the sand from late September to mid-December. The hot summer months, with their high humidity, help incubate the eggs for a period of about 90 days. When the young are ready to hatch, they begin squawking, which signals the mother to open her nest. The young break open their eggs by using a special tooth at the end of their snout.

OPPOSITE The massive hippopotamus spends most of the day submerged beneath the water with just its eyes, ears and nose showing above the surface. It usually exposes its huge teeth and tusks in a display of aggression when threatened.

TOP The remains of various ancient marine fossils have been found on the western shores of Lake St Lucia. These fossils, with intriguing names such ammonites, belemnites and echinoderms, indicate that the area was submerged beneath the sea about 140 million years ago.

ABOVE Ezemvelo KZN Wildlife has established a number of hikes and trails around the lake system of the Greater St Lucia Wetland Park. The diverse habitats attract a variety of birds and animals.

OPPOSITE An aerial view of the estuary mouth shows where it and the Umfolozi River exit into the sea. When the river is in flood large amounts of silt are washed into the ocean.

THESE PAGES Kosi Bay is a unique ecosystem that consists of a series of four lakes. Through the centuries, these lakes have been utilised by the local Tonga people, who have devised an ingenious way of catching fish that has become the largest and most important traditional fishing industry in southern Africa. The reed traps, located mainly in a broad but shallow 5-kilometre channel, form an enclosure that catches the larger fish when the tide recedes. In fact, some 90 per cent of the fish caught in this way are marine species.

BELOW Between October and February every year, female leatherback and loggerhead turtles arrive on the Maputaland coast to nest. The female emerges from the sea at night and lumbers her way up the sand to reach the high-water mark to dig her nest and lay her eggs. After an incubation of some 65 days, the eggs hatch and the young run the gauntlet of various predators as they make their way to the sea. Those that reach the sea are swept by currents to the south, where they take some 12 to 15 years to reach maturity.

OPPOSITE Large numbers of visitors are attracted to Sodwana Bay each year. Not only does it have spectacular white beaches but it is also a divers' paradise, its reef teeming with a veritable kaleidoscope of vividly coloured fish, rays, sharks and some 95 species of coral. The fishing is excellent from both sea and shore, and boats for deep-sea angling and game-fishing are regularly launched on the beachfront.

THESE PAGES Ndumo Game Reserve, in the far north of the province, lies in the floodplain of the Pongola River. There are large stands of fig trees and fever trees and it has a number of fair-sized pans, the Nyamithi Pan being perhaps the most spectacular. Ndumo is a bird-watchers' paradise – not only are there many water birds but also several species that are at the most southern limit of their range. Both hippo and crocodile inhabit the pans and there is a variety of antelope, black and white rhino, as well as a good population of giraffe.

LEFT The sycamore fig is frequently found along the banks of rivers and water courses. It has a bulky yellow trunk, with spreading branches, and the high nutritional value of its leaves and thick clusters of fruit attract a variety of birds and animals.

BELOW Waterbuck are always found near water, favouring areas with tall grass and woodland. They have coarse hair, which is oily, as well as a characteristic white ring on the rump. Only the males have horns.

OPPOSITE Impala both browse and graze and the fruit beneath this sycamore fig provides a tasty meal. The figs ripen between July and December and fall to the ground or are dislodged by monkeys or baboons.

PREVIOUS PAGES Summer evenings in Mkhuze bring respite from
the searing heat of the long days. The bush seems to come alive
in anticipation of cooler times as the sun dips behind the horizon.
LEFT 'King of the Beasts', the lion is the largest African cat and
also the most sociable. It occurs in prides, or family groups, the
size of which varies from five to 12 animals or more. Lions are
extremely territorial.
ABOVE Nyala are shy and secretive and occur in small herds, usually
in woodland thickets. The male is dark grey with a beard and
horns, while the female is chestnut in colour. Both have white
stripes over the back.
OPPOSITE The giraffe, with its long elegant neck and legs, is the
tallest mammal. Its height and excellent eyesight give it the edge
when on the lookout for predators or reaching for leaves in trees.

ABOVE The shallow Nsumu Pan in the Mkhuze Game Reserve is edged with waterlilies and is particularly beautiful in the late afternoon. The birdlife here is prolific and large numbers of flamingo and pelican (both white and pinkbacked) frequent the pan. Hundreds of spurwinged geese and knobbilled duck can also be seen, although they are seasonal visitors. There are two bird-viewing hides that overlook the water.

OPPOSITE Burchell's zebra, with their characteristic black and white stripes, are a common sight in KwaZulu-Natal's game reserves. A breeding herd usually consists of several mares and a single stallion, while young males come together in bachelor herds. Zebra are particularly nervous animals and when startled or threatened they give a sharp alarm call and gallop off in a tight group. They are grazers and are frequently spotted in grasslands and savanna.

BELOW Adjacent to Mkhuze Game Reserve is the scenically splendid Phinda Resource Reserve. Privately owned, it boasts several luxury lodges and offers an up-market wildlife safari with morning and evening game drives in open four-wheel-drive vehicles.

BOTTOM Phinda's lodges are all built with an eye to showcasing the surrounding terrain to its fullest. Guests can enjoy views of riverine woodland, savanna or bushveld, with numerous comforts and amenities to make their experience memorable.

OPPOSITE The cheetah is the most elegant of cats, its long legs and lithe body enabling it to sprint at an incredible 100 kilometres per hour. It prefers a habitat of open plains, with some protective cover for hunting or hiding from other predators. A cheetah has so-called 'tear stains' that run from the inside of each eye to the outer corner of the lips.

LEFT Leopards are solitary animals and have an exceptional skill when it comes to hunting. They are completely at home in trees and use the height to look out for potential prey or enjoy the breeze during the heat of the day.

BELOW Although the boomslang (meaning 'tree snake') is shy, it bites easily and its venom can lead to death in one to three days. The reptile is widespread throughout KwaZulu-Natal and is usually active during the day, when it hunts small birds and chameleons. It lays about 25 eggs during the summer months.

OPPOSITE The large 'warts' on each side of a warthog's face give this species its name. Its canine teeth develop into two curved tusks that are particularly long in the boar and are used for digging up roots and tubers, as well as for self-defence. Warthog families are small.

ABOVE Tembe Elephant Park butts up against South Africa's border with Mozambique and was established to protect the last remaining herds of elephant that migrate between the two countries. The closed woodland and dense thicket that cover most of the reserve can make game-viewing difficult but the hide on the Muzi swamp attracts many species of game as well as prolific birdlife. The reserve is renowned for its especially large elephant.

OPPOSITE Elephant both graze and browse and spend most of their waking hours feeding. Their diet consists largely of grass, bark and leaves, and they are known to walk long distances to reach their favourite food. During the rainy season, they appear to prefer a variety of green grasses. Elephant are active during the day and the night and usually make their way to water holes to drink and bathe in the late afternoon.

PREVIOUS PAGES Durban's beaches are wide and sandy, with shark nets and life savers offering safe swimming to the many sun worshippers that flock here. But there is much more to do than just laze in the sun. Fishing, surfing, paddle-skiing, kite sailing, windsurfing, cycling, walking, eating and shopping all add to the happy buzz of people having fun in and around the beachfront.

OPPOSITE The small craft harbour at the Victoria Embankment is perhaps at its most spectacular just after sunset, when the sky changes to indigo and the city lights are turned on. Several high-end restaurants have outside decks, with bars and dining tables that look out over the quays. A few boats take trips into the bay, the 'booze cruise' in the early evening being particularly popular.

BELOW LEFT The Hari Krishna Temple of Understanding in Chatsworth is a fascinating place. It has an impressive domed ceiling and elaborate altar, the care and devotion given to the various deities seated on it instantly apparent. Decorated with garlands, they are presented with food several times a day, during a ceremony that is accompanied by singing and chanting.

BELOW RIGHT It is estimated that some 87 per cent of South Africa's Indian population resides in KwaZulu-Natal. A large number belong to the Hindu faith, their beliefs given expression in various colourful ceremonies. A Hindu wedding is especially elaborate, the bride usually dressed in a fabulous sari and traditional jewellery.

THESE PAGES Recently constructed near the harbour mouth, uShaka Marine World is an enormous theme park that houses the largest aquarium in the southern hemisphere and offers various thrilling water rides and activities. The aquarium is ingeniously built beneath and around the creaking decks and leaking cabins of a supposed sunken ship. A variety of sharks, rays, huge turtles, vibrantly coloured fish and a myriad other sea life can be seen in the massive tanks that are guaranteed to enthral even the most cynical visitor. At the dolphinarium, the daily shows of performing bottlenosed dolphins, African penguins and Cape fur seals lure both young and old alike, and the squeals of delight as these incredible creatures go through their paces attest to their skill. The aquarium and dolphinarium aside, there are numerous restaurants, art galleries and shops within the uShaka complex.

OPPOSITE Fishermen haul in their nets on the Durban beachfront. This is one of the few remaining operations of this type, as most fishermen now use boats with outboard motors. BELOW AND BOTTOM In June/July every year millions of sardines migrate up the South Coast and 'sardine fever' grips the public. For some it is a serious commercial opportunity, for others simply a chance to have some fun.

TOP LEFT The Victoria Street Market, in the old quarter of Durban, is a labyrinth of tiny shops that seem to sell anything and everything. Brassware, African and Asian artifacts, rugs, clothing, pots, pans, herbs and curry powders adorn every available space in a glorious array of colour.

LEFT A ricksha ride is an absolute must on a trip to Durban. Dressed in elaborately beaded tunics and headdresses, drivers run and leap to the delight of their passengers.

ABOVE The Juma Mosque in Grey Street is a famous landmark known for its golden dome and turrets. Its cool interior is a stark contrast to the bustling streets outside.

OPPOSITE An aerial view of Durban's 'Golden Mile' shows luxury hotels and apartments with superb views over the Indian Ocean. The pier is one of several in Durban bay.

OVERLEAF Most of the larger golf courses hire out golf carts, clubs and caddies, and also boast various practice facilities. Courses in KwaZulu-Natal range through parkland, links and mountain, and stands of indigenous bush attract a prolific birdlife. It is not uncommon for golfers to encounter various small antelope. Sea breezes and humidity add to the challenge at coastal venues, while winter frost changes the fairways to brown in the Drakensberg.

OPPOSITE The Zimbali Golf Course on the North Coast is one of the most challenging in the country as it moves from sweeping contoured fairways to undulating greens. The clubhouse and lodge are superb and the estate has magnificent views over the Indian Ocean.

ABOVE The province is renowned for its excellent golf courses and the generally pleasant weather means that golfing enthusiasts can indulge themselves year round. The Umdoni Park Golf Course is located on the South Coast and takes its name from the many umdoni trees that grow there.

RIGHT South Africa's first golf estate, Selborne Golf Course on the South Coast, was established in the 1980s. Like many courses, it is located in an area of great natural beauty.

LEFT The coastal town of Margate offers affordable getaways for families, and during the peak season in April, July and December the town almost bursts at the seams with holidaymakers. It is particularly geared for the young, and street markets, beach events, beauty competitions and music concerts are organised for these periods. Margate's long beach has shark nets and there are life savers on duty.

BELOW Margate also caters for fishermen, with several well-placed piers not far from the main beach. The fishing is good, although as the sun sets at the end of a balmy day and the waves break against the rocks below, perhaps it is the experience and not the fish that make the occasion.

OPPOSITE Like Margate, the little town of Ramsgate boasts a Blue Flag beach, indicating that it is of a particularly high standard and meets certain international criteria of excellence. The beach is fringed with palm trees and is located in a very attractive bay with a lagoon.

TOP LEFT Just west of Port Shepstone lies the spectacular Oribi Gorge. Some of the huge sandstone cliffs found here are over 360 metres high and drop dramatically down to the uMzimkulwana River below. These rugged cliffs are home to troops of baboon, their harsh calls echoing out across the gorge. Seven species of eagle soar above the crags and leopard are sometimes seen among the rocks.

ABOVE There are various viewing points with spectacular vistas over the gorge and forested slopes to the river. These spots include Overhanging Rock, Baboon's Castle and The Pulpit. Hiking and horse riding are popular pastimes and avid birdwatchers and nature lovers are enticed by an extensive bird population and possible glimpses of vervet and samango monkeys, reedbuck, bushbuck and the blue and common duiker.

LEFT The area is renowned for its 'Wild Five' adventure sports – the swing, abseil, slide, white-water rafting and mountain biking. The swing requires one to leap off a cliff, attached to a harness and a cable strung across the gorge, approximately 160 metres above the river bed below.

OPPOSITE The Oribi Gorge Nature Reserve, managed by Ezemvelo KZN Wildlife, has several stunning waterfalls that cascade over the rocks into tranquil pools surrounded by lush vegetation. Indigenous trees and plants form cool green glades that invite hikers to pause and enjoy their splendour.

THESE PAGES The Midmar Dam is located near Howick in the KwaZulu-Natal Midlands. The dam, some 1 800 hectares in extent, is a popular venue for yachting and other water sports and for those who just wish to laze around on its grassy banks. It hosts the annual Midmar Mile, a gruelling swim that attracts thousands of entrants each year. There is a range of chalets for hire as well as several camp sites.

LEFT The Midlands is quite a locale for adventure sports, the natural beauty of the surrounds lending itself to a variety of outdoor activities. The huge trees in the indigenous forests of the Karkloof gave birth to the Karkloof Canopy Tours, where adrenalin junkies hurtle along a series of cables strung between the tree tops.

BELOW Canoeing has a large following in the area, helped by the availability of several fast-flowing rivers. The Dusi Canoe Marathon is an annual three-day event that starts in Pietermaritzburg on the uMsunduzi River and finishes at the mouth of the uMngeni River in Durban. Competition is intense and the event attracts contestants from around the world.

PREVIOUS PAGES The Midlands is farming country and cattle, horses, sheep and goats are as much part of the landscape as lush pastures and farm dams. Driving along the winding roads, visitors can slow down a pace, breathe in the fresh air and enjoy the country experience. There are numerous places to eat, buy farm produce or browse through an array of local arts and crafts.

OPPOSITE The Howick Falls, focal point of the town of Howick, plunge about 100 metres into the gorge below. Over the years, various myths and legends have been woven around these falls and, according to Zulu folklore, an ancestral spirit in the form of a huge snake resides in the pool below, and can occasionally be seen near the surface.

PREVIOUS PAGES Located in the foothills of the southern Drakensberg, the quaint village of Underberg makes an ideal base from which to explore the area. The trout fishing is particularly good here – so much so that the Underberg/Himeville Trout Fishing Club manages some 170 kilometres of rivers and no fewer than 60 dams.

LEFT Jacob's Ladder Falls in the Lotheni Nature Reserve in the southern Drakensberg flows over a series of steps in a glorious cascade. Situated in the Little 'Berg, the reserve is scenically spectacular, its grassy slopes home to numerous antelope, including eland, mountain reedbuck and common duiker.

ABOVE The Gaudy Commodore (*Junonia octavia sesamus*) is an especially striking resident of the Drakensberg mountain range.

OPPOSITE Rainbow Gorge in the Cathedral Peak area is long and narrow and when conditions are right the spray from its many falls and rapids drifts upwards, creating glorious rainbows against the light.

ABOVE While snow does fall on the high peaks of the Drakensberg during the winter months, it is not all that usual for it to reach the foothills of the mountains to any great extent. It is quite an occasion when snow actually carpets the ground in deep drifts as it has on this road between the village of Nottingham Road and the Lotheni Nature Reserve. The landscape was altered completely, transformed into a winter wonderland overnight.

OPPOSITE These fields are usually a sea of lush green where cattle graze peacefully under the sun and the farms are a hive of activity with workers and vehicles always on the go. Now covered in thick snow, the countryside looks deserted, with no signs of life anywhere.

LEFT The Cathedral Peak region in the central Drakensberg offers a range of hikes that vary from easy to the extreme. The scenery is dramatic, with towering rock faces, grassy slopes and stands of indigenous forest. There is some outstanding San rock art in the area, particularly at Ndedema Gorge, and the San Art Centre at Didima Camp provides a fascinating audiovisual presentation of San culture.

ABOVE Isolated against a backdrop of the mountains, Meander Hut at Giant's Castle offers rustic overnight accommodation to hikers. It is perched at the edge of a cliff and looks down over the Meander Stream, which cuts a winding path through the scenery. Giant's Castle boasts several herds of eland, and hikers are likely to see one or more of these huge antelope.

OPPOSITE While Lotheni Nature Reserve is most renowned for its excellent trout fishing and easy rambles, it also provides a convenient base for the serious hiker and mountaineer to tackle the high peaks known as The Hawk and The Tent, as well as several other lesser-known rock faces that soar to well over 3 000 metres. Accommodation in Lotheni includes thatched chalets and a caravan and camping site.

BELOW Cobham in the southern Drakensberg is a favourite with both hikers and fishermen, lured to the area by the numerous hiking trails and good trout-fishing spots. Situated on the banks of the Pholela River, Cobham is extremely picturesque and is an overnight stop on the five-day Giant's Cup Hiking Trail, the view towards Giant's Cup being particularly spectacular from the camp. The many rivers and streams and countless ponds in the valley attract large numbers of water birds and several species of antelope.

OPPOSITE Champagne Valley is the most popular holiday area of the Drakensberg and offers a wide range of accommodation and recreational facilities, notably the spectacular golf course at the Champagne Valley Sports Resort, which has wonderful views of the surrounding mountains. Several peaks dominate the area – Cathkin Peak, Champagne Castle, the Dragon's Back and Monk's Cowl, the latter representing the greatest challenge to mountaineers in the Drakensberg. The valley is home to the world-famous Drakensberg Boys' Choir and their performances are a huge tourist attraction.

LEFT Fields of arum lilies are a common sight in the marshy areas of the Little 'Berg. They are surprisingly resilient and can tolerate very cold weather and even snow.

BELOW White scilla occur in the grassland areas, their flowers bunched tightly together at first but opening as their stems lengthen between September and February.

BOTTOM Hairbells, or wand-flowers, which occur in the grasslands, hang delicately from slender stalks.

OPPOSITE The woody Drakensberg sugarbush has successfully adapted to fire.

LEFT The various shapes and sizes of stone, rock and buttress in the Drakensberg have given rise to many apt names and none more so than the Policeman's Helmet at the Royal Natal National Park. The hike to the Helmet is surprisingly arduous, as the path is very steep.

BELOW A glimpse of the shy serval is a special treat. This dainty predator prefers areas near water with thick reeds or grass for cover. It is solitary and has acute hearing, hunting for insects, birds and small rodents at night.

OPPOSITE The Amphitheatre at the Royal Natal National Park is, for many, the icon of the Drakensberg. It is a spectacular wall of rock that is some 5 kilometres long and the mighty Thukela River rises on the summit at Mont-aux-Sources.

PREVIOUS PAGES The Zulu name for Cathkin Peak is *Mdedelelo*, meaning 'the bully', which is entirely appropriate – despite the fact that it is not as high as its neighbour, it completely dominates the skyline. The massive peaks in this central area lure many a mountaineer, but for lesser mortals several easy walks include Fern Forest, Barry's Grave and the Grotto.

THESE PAGES The magnificent Game Pass Shelter at Kamberg has some of the finest San rock art in southern Africa. The art is a visual documentary of events in the valley over thousands of years, more recently when the San came up against the aggressive cultures of both black and white settlers who moved into the area. At this and other sites, their rock paintings and engravings reveal their gentle way of life and show an intimate knowledge of nature, a reverence for wild animals and an identification of themselves in their environment. Human figures and animals are a common theme and the mythological world is often represented by half-human, half-animal figures. The eland is frequently depicted and it is obvious that it was held in high esteem, not only to hunt but also in their religious beliefs. There is a San Rock Art Interpretation Centre at the camp.

LEFT Fields of agapanthus thrive on the moist lower slopes of the mountain in the Injasuthi area, their dark blue heads providing a flash of colour in the surrounding grasslands. The species is traditionally used as a lucky charm to ward off evil spirits.

ABOVE The Sani Pass, which lies between KwaZulu-Natal and Lesotho, is one of the most impressive mountain passes in southern Africa. It starts gently but soon becomes incredibly steep, rising to 2 874 metres, 1 330 metres of which is climbed in the last 8 kilometres.

OPPOSITE The Sani Pass was named after the San who once lived in the area and for many years it was navigable only by horses and mule trains. In 1955 it was used intermittently by the Mokhotlong Mountain Transport, while today it is a regular route between the two countries.

OVERLEAF The rolling foothills of Giant's Castle are favoured by the eland, and the game reserve was established in 1903 in order to protect these huge antelope. For thousands of years, the San occupied these mountains and left behind a priceless legacy of rock art in numerous caves and overhangs.